The Student Writer's Workshop

Everything You Need for a Successful Student Writer's Workshop

by Megan Chaney

Good Apple
A Division of Frank Schaffer Publications, Inc.

Thank you to my husband, Brian, for the encouragement, patience and support in writing this book.

Special thanks to Cherie Boone for your loving guidance throughout my life.

Dedicated to my former student, Leah Lagueux, a very special and talented young writer who can

> "... hear a rose blooming, hear the day
> rushing into tomorrow, and hear the
> earth growing... I can touch a rainbow... "

I wish for you to keep reaching for those rainbows.

Imprint Manager: Kristin Eclov
Editors: Janet Barker & Cindy Barden
Inside Design: Rose Sheifer Graphic Productions
Cover Design: Rita Hudson
Illustration: Mike Denman

GOOD APPLE
A Division of Frank Schaffer Publications
23740 Hawthorne Boulevard
Torrance, CA 90505

Contents

A Note to Readers

Teachers have frequent opportunities to attend professional workshops on a variety of topics. For students, that option is rarely available. You can make this possible by setting up your own Student Writer's Workshops. Use creative ideas for fun and interactive writer's activities by planning full- or half-day writing workshops for your students.

The activities in this book have been designed to present formal, structured writing through exciting Student Writer's Workshops. When writing is associated with fun activities and experiences, students look forward to writing assignments.

Writing is a skill students will use for a lifetime. Teachers can help them develop this skill through a variety of creative lessons and activities. Formal writing requires specific skills that will enable students to write fluent, mature, and accurate text.

All conceptual text, hands-on activities, and practice activities in this book involve formal text writing. Because students will be expected to do a large amount of writing, it is not necessary that every writing assignment be a polished copy. Students write in rough draft form for most of the activities. If they wish to publish a particular text, they may choose to do so.

Although this book concentrates on formal writing, you can use these strategies as models for setting up writing workshops on other types of writing from poetry to drama, creative writing, speculative fiction, and report writing.

Before you hold your first writing workshop, introduce and/or review "paragraph" writing basics. "Make Way for the Paragraph Train" on page 7 provides a fun way to do this.

Formal/structured writing requires specific organizational skills as well as writing skills. Skills learned in one type of writing, like writing topic sentences, using transitional words, organizing paragraphs, and writing conclusions, are easily transferred to other types of writing. Both creative writing and formal writing skills are useful in life. Ask students for examples of when they might use these skills in school or as adults. Most adults use formal writing skills more often than creative writing. Writing memos, letters

to the editor, letters of explanation, complaint or inquiry, and reports for employers are all types of formal writing used in everyday life.

Early in the year you will want to assess students' writing abilities. The introductions to expository and narrative writing on pages 12 and 13 provide activities for assessment. Narrative and Expository Writing Skills Assessment sheets can be found on pages 58—61.

You'll also find many visual aids for posters and overheads and a wide variety of writing activities to use either as part of your Student Writer's Workshops and/or to incorporate in your daily writing lesson plans.

The activities on pages 39—50 can be incorporated into Student Writer's Workshops or be used as follow-up activities. Other follow-up activities include: "Students as Teachers" and "Night Writes!" To help you and your students reach writing goals, End-of-the-Year Writer's Expectations by grade level are included on pages 62—64.

For teachers to teach effectively, they also need to continue to grow as learners. Creating *The Student' Writer's Workshop* has been a four-year project, a time in which I grew, both as a student, and as an educator. My experience researching and writing this book has convinced me that the more we, as teachers, expand our knowledge of teaching methods, the better educators we become.

You are to be commended. By purchasing this book you have demonstrated a keen desire to expand your teaching repertoire with the implied goal that what you learn today will one day inspire the hearts and minds of children. It is my sincere hope that *The Student Writer's Workshop* helps you share your love of writing with children.

Megan Chaney

Make Way for the Paragraph Train

Purpose: To make an analogy of a paragraph to a train to help students better understand the structure of a paragraph.

This activity is best used prior to the Student Writer's Workshop as a way of introducing or reviewing basic paragraph skills.

Start by asking students questions about trains: Have you ever seen a train go by on a railroad track? What was at the beginning of the train? How many boxcars did you see? What did you notice about the boxcars? What was at the end of the train?

Activate students' prior knowledge about writing paragraphs. Explain how a paragraph has a topic sentence, three or more supporting sentences, and a closing sentence.

How is a Paragraph Like a Train?

The Topic Sentence is like an Engine.

A paragraph has a topic sentence to state or "pull" along the contents in the paragraph like the train has an engine to pull along the cars of the train.

The Supporting Sentences are like Boxcars.

In a paragraph, the supporting sentences are what "holds the cargo" or are the main content of the paragraph. There must be at least three supporting sentences to adequately support the topic sentence.

A train has boxcars that carry its cargo. The boxcars make up the bulk of the train just like the supporting sentences do for the paragraph.

The Closing Sentence is like a Caboose.

The closing sentence ends the paragraph, like the caboose signals the end of the train. After the analogy is understood, model the train activity on page 8.

Paragraph Train Activity

Purpose: To model the analogy of how a paragraph is like a train and provide manipulatives for students to do the same.

This activity can be completed before introducing the Student Writer's Workshop. The patterns can be used as visual aids during the Writer's Workshop to review and reinforce what students have already learned.

Use the train patterns on pages 9—12 to make manipulatives for each student. Photocopy the patterns onto different colored paper and have students cut them out. The patterns will be more durable if you laminate them before cutting.

When each student has a set of the train manipulatives, demonstrate how to use them for this activity.

Set up the train starting with the engine, three boxcars, and the caboose—in that order—on the right side of your desk. As you write a topic sentence, move the engine of the train, which represents the topic sentence, to the left.

As you continue modeling the writing process, continue to move the boxcars, and finally, the caboose.

After you model this activity, students can practice writing paragraphs using the manipulatives.

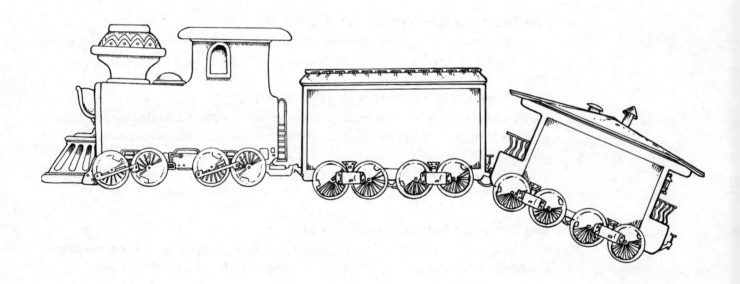

Paragraph Train Activity Patterns

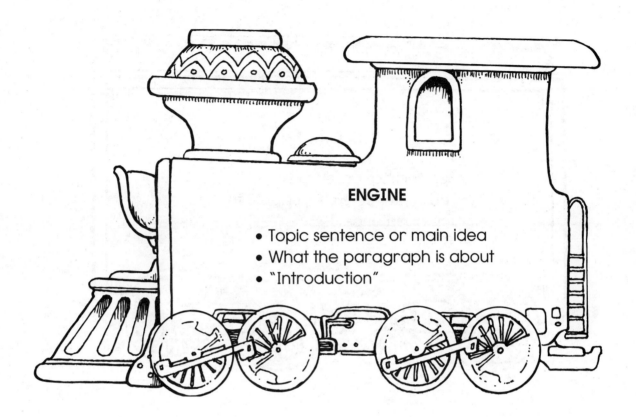

ENGINE

- Topic sentence or main idea
- What the paragraph is about
- "Introduction"

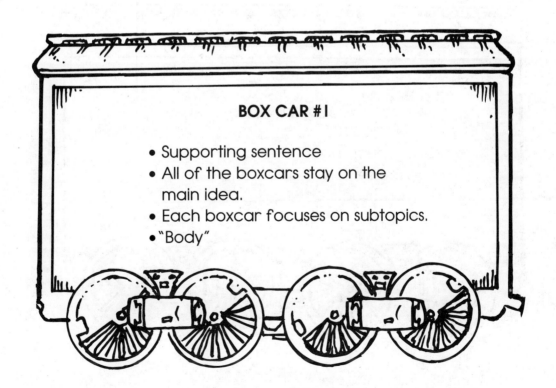

BOX CAR #1

- Supporting sentence
- All of the boxcars stay on the main idea.
- Each boxcar focuses on subtopics.
- "Body"

Reproducible

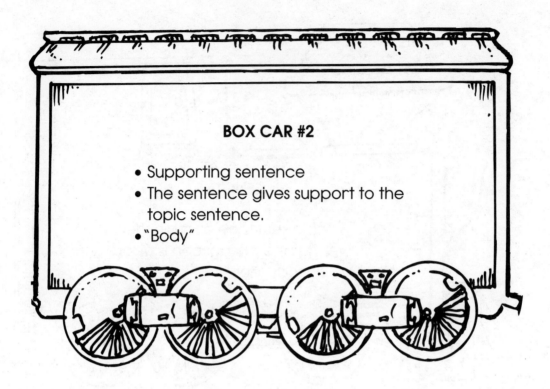

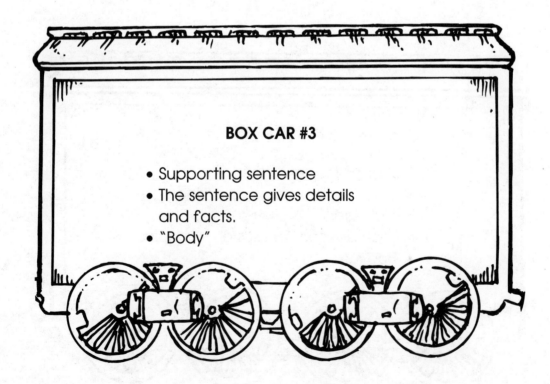

Reproducible

Paragraph Train Activity Patterns

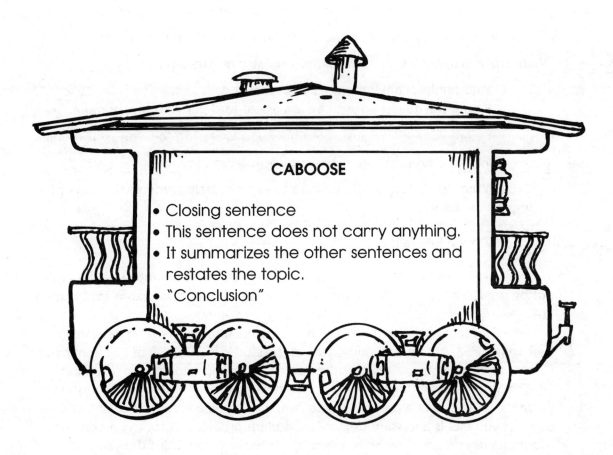

CABOOSE

- Closing sentence
- This sentence does not carry anything.
- It summarizes the other sentences and restates the topic.
- "Conclusion"

　　　Reproducible

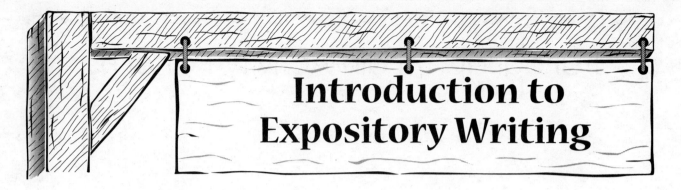

Introduction to Expository Writing

Purpose: To introduce and/or review expository writing to the class and to provide the teacher with a means of assessing students' writing abilities.

This activity can be used in advance of the Student Writer's Workshop.

 WRITE THE FOLLOWING EXPOSITORY WRITING PROMPT ON THE BOARD:

Your family is having guests this weekend.
Before the guests arrive, you are asked to clean your messy room.

 Before you write, think about how you are going to clean your room.

Write an explanation of how you will clean your room.

Explain that expository writing means to explain. Help students remember by writing on the board:

 EX-pository = EX-plain

Explain that this writing activity will be used as an assessment tool. They will not be graded on it. The purpose is to get an overview of their expository writing skills.

When students finish writing, use the Student Expository Writing Assessment tool on page 58. Return the assignment to the students with one or two comments. Be sure to include at least one positive comment for each student.

The Student Expository Writing Skills Assessment page is designed to assess students' writing over a period of time. You may complete an assessment as often as you feel is necessary to monitor student progress. This can be done on spontaneous writing activities or on assigned topics throughout the year.

The first time you fill in the student assessment sheet, use a colored pen or highlighter to write the date, circle the appropriate skill level, and make notes about items to praise and areas you need to work on with the student. Each succeeding time you assess the student, use a different color pen or highlighter to write the date, circle the appropriate skill level, and make notes. This will give you a visual, "at-a glance" record of student progress. You may choose to share this assessment record with students or parents on a quarterly basis.

"Ice Cream Sundaes" (page 19) can be used as an introductory expository writing activity. See the "Flowchart for Expository Writing" (page 21) and "Steps for Writing Expository Text" (page 22) for other material you can use to teach expository writing.

Introduction to Narrative Writing

Purpose: To introduce and/or review narrative writing to the class and to provide the teacher with a means of assessing student writing abilities.

This activity can be used in advance of the Student Writer's Workshop.

 WRITE THE FOLLOWING NARRATIVE WRITING PROMPT ON THE BOARD:

Many people like to watch movies.
What if you were able to meet your favorite movie star?

 Before you begin to write, think about which movie star you would like to meet.

Tell a story about meeting your favorite movie star.

Explain that narrative writing means to tell a story. Sometimes the story is about something that actually happened. It also could be about something that might have happened, or something that might happen in the future.

Have students write their names and the date on a sheet of notebook paper. Explain that this writing activity will be used as an assessment tool. They will not be graded on it. The purpose is to get an overview of their narrative writing skills.

When students finish writing, use the Student Narrative Writing Assessment tool on page 60. Return the assignment to the students with one or two comments. Be sure to include at least one positive comment for each student.

The Student Narrative Writing Skills Assessment page is designed to assess students' writing over a period of time. You may complete an assessment as often as you feel is necessary to monitor student progress. This can be done on spontaneous writing activities or on assigned topics throughout the year.

The first time you fill in the student assessment sheet, use a colored pen or highlighter to write the date, circle the appropriate skill level, and make notes about items to praise and areas you need to work on with the student. Each succeeding time you assess the student, use a different color pen or highlighter to write the date, circle the appropriate skill level, and make notes. This will give you a visual, "at-a glance" record of student progress. You may choose to share this assessment record with students or parents on a quarterly basis.

"Candy Characters" (page 19) can be used as an introductory narrative writing activity. See the "Narrative Writing Organizer" (page 23) and "Steps for Writing Narrative Text" (page 24) for other material you can use to teach narrative writing.

Planning Student Writer's Workshops

Advance Planning is the Key

Plan the Student Writer's Workshop similar to workshops teachers attend. Like teachers, students enjoy a break from their normal routine. With proper advance planning on your part, this can be a fun and educational experience for students.

- Build curiosity for the Student Writer's Workshop by hanging signs and posters around the room to "advertise" the event.

- Involve students from the beginning by having them contribute to the sign and poster making during art classes.

- Post a countdown to the big day.

- Let students know this day will be their day to attend a "professional" workshop like teachers do.

- Post a written agenda of the workshop in advance.

- Make Student Writer's Workshops opportunities for new learning experiences.

- Provide notepads, pens, or other writing-related freebies to participants.

- Provide specific times for students to socialize during breaks.

- Provide snacks between workshop sessions.

- If possible, have at least one guest speaker for one of the writing sessions.

- If you have other volunteers who will be giving writing sessions during the workshop, offer students the option of attending alternate sessions.

- Create a writing workshop atmosphere by using many visual aids.

- Hold some writing sessions outside your classroom.

- Include a student critique after the workshop.

Who Will You Invite as a Guest Speaker?

You could invite a professor from a nearby college or a local author who has published children's books as a guest speaker. A librarian, journalist, or other person who works in a writing-related field would also be a welcome guest.

Contact other teachers in your school to see if they will agree to participate. Two classes could be combined for a writing workshop. That would enable you and the other teacher to offer more variety.

Do you have parent volunteers or classroom assistants that could hold one session of the workshop? Perhaps the physical education teacher would conduct a short sports-writing session. How about the school nurse? Expose students to a variety of people, professions and writing opportunities.

Where Will You Hold Your Workshop Sessions?

If possible, plan to hold at least some of the sessions in rooms outside the regular classroom. If you were planning a nature writing activity, students might sit outside for that session, weather permitting. For a food-related writing activity, the cafeteria might be ideal. A sports-related writing activity might take place in the gym.

Check to see which areas are available for use. The library, auditorium, or even a hallway may work for short sessions. Pushing all the desks to one side of the room and sitting on a blanket on the floor gives students an opportunity for something out of the ordinary routine.

How Will You Provide Writing-Related Items and Snacks for Students Without Spending a Lot of Money?

Prior to the workshop, ask local merchants for donations of pens, notepads, and other writing-related materials. Many merchants are more than willing to help out, especially if the material they provide advertises their business in some way. Also ask for donations for food and drink items, and/or small items that could be used as door prizes. Free food or drink coupons from fast food or pizza restaurants are an option for door prizes.

Parents may be willing to donate cookies or other food and drink items. Some snacks, like popcorn, a large bag of animal crackers, and fruit drinks are quite inexpensive, even for an entire class. A letter to parents in advance usually brings a positive response.

What About Visuals for the Writer's Workshop?

Prepare visuals in advance and place them around the room on the day of the workshop. Photocopy the items suggested below on brightly colored paper. Use photographs or posters related to scheduled writing topics.

Paragraph Train patterns from pages 9—11 enlarged and cut from brightly colored posterboard

Flowchart for Expository Writing on page 21

Steps for Writing Expository Text visual aid on page 22

Narrative Writing Organizer (BME) on page 23

Steps for Writing Narrative Text visual aid on page 24

Expository Prompt Clue Words visual aid on page 30

Narrative Prompt Clue Words visual aid on page 31

Attention Grabbers visual aid on page 34

Transitions visual aid on page 35

Instead of Writing Said... visual aid on page 36

The End and No Erase signs on pages 37 and 38

Start Your Writer's Workshop Off With a Smile

When students enter the class for the Student Writer's Workshop, welcome them with a smile as they sign in at the "registration desk" staffed by student volunteers. Give each student a small gift when they register (pen, pencil, notepad, keychain, etc.).

If you have obtained appropriate donated items from local merchants, give each student a half numbered ticket at registration. Put the other half in a box. Hold several drawings for small door prizes at various intervals during the day.

Let students relax during a 10 to 15 minute social time with juice and cookies or mini-muffins before getting down to work. The atmosphere of the room should be language and print rich. The ambiance should be comfortable and free of

16

pressure. While you are instructing, allow students to quietly get up and help themselves to more snacks.

Invite students to take notes simply by saying, "Today you are attending a workshop like teachers attend. When you hear something interesting or you think a particular point is important, take notes like teachers do at workshops." Most students will help themselves to the free pens and notepads and get into the spirit of the day.

Suggested Activities

Use these ideas, combined with your own, to make your Student Writer's Workshop a fun-filled day of learning.

How to Read and Write Prompts on pages 25 and 26 (include the overhead on page 27 and student activity on page 28).

Focus Scope writing activity on page 39

I Spy Riddle Game writing activity on page 41

Paper Bag Topic Game writing activity on page 42

Rotating Group Paragraph writing activity on page 44

The Great Pet Escape writing activity on page 46

What's Inside the Hat? writing activity on page 48

Have a fun time at your Student Workshop Day!

Follow-up

Use the follow-up activity, "Students as Teachers," on page 51 to reinforce the content presented during the workshop.

Make copies for each student of the evaluation form on page 18. Ask students to fill out the evaluation at the end of the Writer's Workshop, or the next day.

Student Evaluation

Did you enjoy attending the Writer's Workshop? Why or why not?

_____

_____

_____

What part of the Writer's Workshop did you like best? Why?

_____

_____

_____

What part of the Writer's Workshop did you like least? Why?

_____

_____

_____

Would you like to have another Writer's Workshop? Why or why not?

_____

_____

_____

If you could change one thing about the Writer's Workshop to make it better, what would you change?

_____

_____

_____

Reproducible

Yummy Writing

Purpose: To introduce students to expository and narrative writing.

These activities can be used in advance of the Student Writer's Workshop or as part of the Workshop itself.

Ice Cream Sundaes: Expository Essay Writing

Ice cream is a special treat that children just can't resist. When ice cream and writing are combined into a lesson, you are going to get some tasty results. The students will unknowingly transfer the positive and happy feelings of eating ice cream to writing an essay.

You can make and eat the sundaes before you write or you can do this after you write. Making the sundaes first and writing afterwards provides the students with "fresh and cool" details to include in their essay. Making the sundaes last and writing first can help students realize important details they forgot in their essay,

Either way you decide to do this activity, it is guaranteed to be successful!

Candy Characters: Narrative Story Writing

Almost everyone loves to eat candy! In this activity, candy is associated with writing by using favorite candies for the characters, setting, and action.

Use candy with appropriate names that can be used in a story like 3 Musketeers™, Baby Ruth™, Mr. Goodbar™, Milky Way™, Starburst™, etc.

Unwrap the candy and put it in small sandwich bags for students to eat after completing the activity. Use the wrappers as a border and glue them on an 11" x 17" (27 cm x 43.2 cm) sheet of lined paper. Use this as a master and make photocopies for each student.

Explain to students that they will pick their characters, setting, and action from the names of candy to write their stories. They can use the names of real candy products, or make up their own, like Peter Peppermint or Lisa Lemondrop.

While they write, walk around the room to offer assistance and make observations. When the rough draft is completed, provide time for students to share their stories—and the candy.

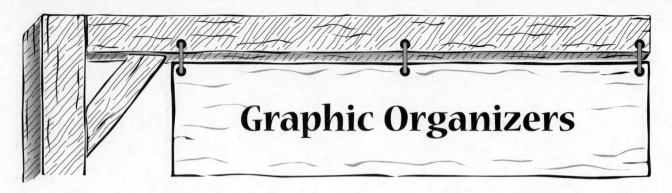

Graphic Organizers

Purpose: To provide visuals for structuring narrative and expository writing.

This material can be used after the initial student assessment writing assignment and/or as part of the Student Writer's Workshop.

Expository Writing Organizers

When students write formal text, which is structured writing, their graphic organizers also need to be structured. To explain expository writing, use the flowchart on page 21. This highly structured format is used because this type of text needs to be very organized. The flowchart shows students exactly what needs to go into each section of their essays.

Make a copy of the Flowchart for Expository Writing for each student. Model a sample of expository writing as you discuss each step in the chart. Students can use this flowchart throughout the year for expository writing activities.

Make a copy of the Steps for Writing Expository Text on page 22 to use on the overhead projector. As you explain each step, model a sample of expository writing with the class. Ask students to give examples related to the topic for each step.

Narrative Writing Organizers

As you explain narrative writing, students will find the Narrative Writing Organizer on page 23 very useful. Make a copy for each student. Model a sample of narrative writing as you discuss each section of the organizer. Students can continue to use this organizer throughout the year for narrative writing activities.

The Steps for Writing Narrative Text on page 24 is another useful visual aid. Make a copy to use on the overhead projector. As you explain each step, model a sample of narrative writing with the class. Ask students to give examples related to the topic for each step.

Plan to spend a full week on expository writing and another full week on narrative writing. To avoid confusion, students should not practice both skills at the same time until they can apply the skills and concepts accurately.

Once they have learned both types of writing, students should be able to distinguish between expository and narrative writing and apply the appropriate skills.

Flowchart for Expository Writing

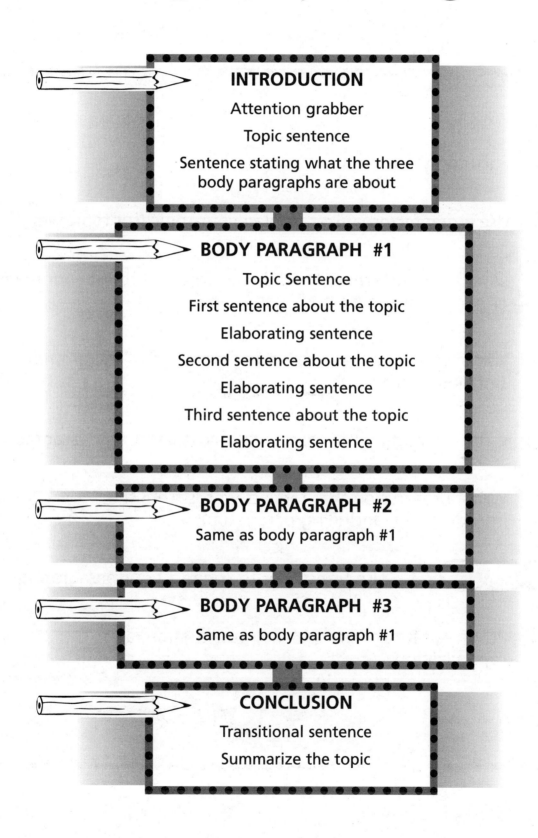

INTRODUCTION

Attention grabber

Topic sentence

Sentence stating what the three body paragraphs are about

BODY PARAGRAPH #1

Topic Sentence

First sentence about the topic

Elaborating sentence

Second sentence about the topic

Elaborating sentence

Third sentence about the topic

Elaborating sentence

BODY PARAGRAPH #2

Same as body paragraph #1

BODY PARAGRAPH #3

Same as body paragraph #1

CONCLUSION

Transitional sentence

Summarize the topic

Steps for Writing Expository Text

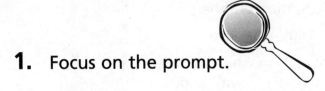

1. Focus on the prompt.

2. Use a graphic organizer to plan your topic (subtopic web).

3. Brainstorm at least three subtopics about your main topic (three body paragraphs).

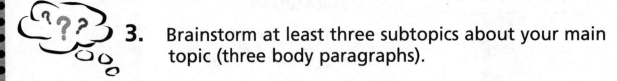

4. Write a topic sentence repeating words from the prompt (introduction).

5. Write a paragraph for each subtopic (three body paragraphs).

6. Write a conclusion that repeats words from the introduction (concluding paragraph).

7. Use transitions to connect your paragraphs.

8. Proofread for correct spelling, punctuation, and capitalization.

Reproducible

Narrative Writing Organizer

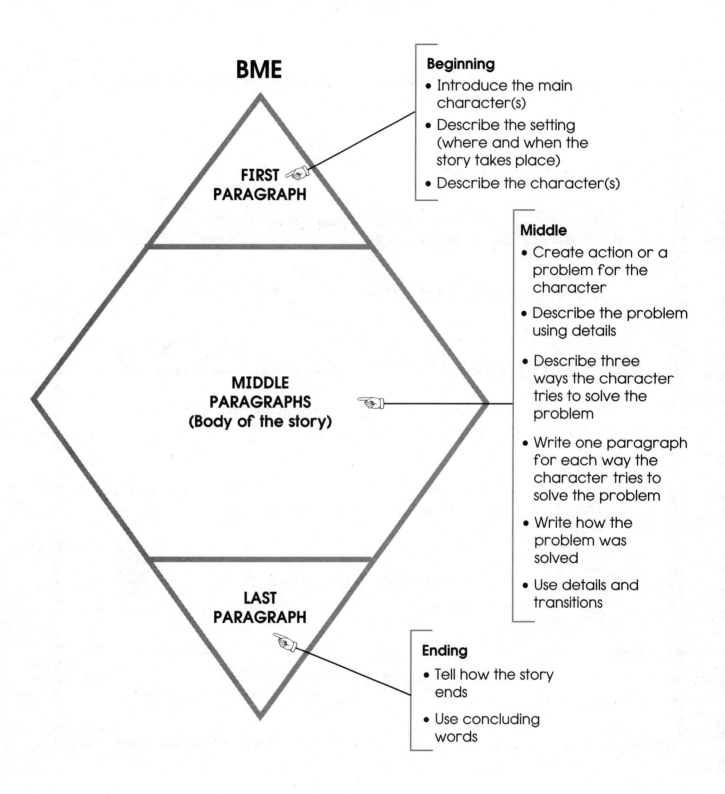

BME

FIRST PARAGRAPH

Beginning
- Introduce the main character(s)
- Describe the setting (where and when the story takes place)
- Describe the character(s)

MIDDLE PARAGRAPHS (Body of the story)

Middle
- Create action or a problem for the character
- Describe the problem using details
- Describe three ways the character tries to solve the problem
- Write one paragraph for each way the character tries to solve the problem
- Write how the problem was solved
- Use details and transitions

LAST PARAGRAPH

Ending
- Tell how the story ends
- Use concluding words

Steps for Writing Narrative Text

1. Focus on the prompt.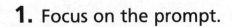

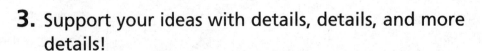

2. Use a graphic organizer to plan your ideas (beginning, middle, end).

3. Support your ideas with details, details, and more details!

4. Use transitions to connect your ideas.

5. Be creative with the words used in your story. Don't use the same words over and over again.

6. Write a closing sentence at the end of the story instead of writing THE END. Do not write THE END.

7. Proofread for correct spelling, punctuation, and capitalization.

© Good Apple GA1681

How to Read and Write Prompts

Purpose: To teach students to understand the three parts of a prompt and to identify clue words in a prompt.

This activity can be used during the Student Writer's Workshop or at any time early in the year.

Students need to know how to read and understand prompts in order to perform well in their writing. Teaching them the "secrets" to reading and understanding prompts will insure student success with writing when they apply what they learned.

Three Sections of a Prompt

Tell students there are three sections to prompts and each section has a specific purpose. Make an overhead of the prompts on page 27. Read the first prompt out loud and point out each of the three sections as you explain the purpose of each section.

Section 1: The scenario.
Explain that this is the background information they need to know before they begin to write. Ask students why they think this is important information.

Section 2: Think about it.
Students need to think about what they are going to write before they actually start writing. Ask students why it's important to spend time thinking before they begin writing. Is thinking wasted time? Why not simply jump in and begin writing immediately?

Section 3: Directions on how to write the text.
This section tells students what type of writing they will be doing; whether they will be writing expository or narrative text.

The third section contains words that tell them what type of writing they will be doing. For expository writing, look for words like *explain, tell why,* and *tell how.* For narrative writing, watch for words like *tell a story, write a story,* and *tell about.*

Remind students that expository writing means they will explain something.

EXpository = EXplain

Narrative means they will tell a story about something that has happened, might have happened, or could happen in the future.

Ask students whether they would be doing expository or narrative writing for the first example on the overhead.

Read the rest of the prompts out loud as a class. Have students point out the three sections for each prompt. Ask students to determine whether they would be writing expository or narrative text for each prompt.

Clue Words

Tell students that clue words are the key to knowing what the focus of their writing will be. Go back to the first prompt and show students how to recognize clue words. Tell them that usually the clue words are repeated in all three sections. Point out and circle the clue words "prepare dinner" in each section of the first prompt. Ask students why they think the clue words are important. How do clue words help us focus on the topic?

As students identify clue words in the other prompts, circle the clue words so they stand out. It will be easier for students to stay focused if they identify and circle clue words before they begin to write.

Using Clue Words

Students need to realize that the repeated words used as clues in the prompts need to be repeated in their text to show that they are focused on the topic. Tell students that using the clue words in a sentence may be the best way to start an essay.

Point again to the first prompt on the overhead. Ask several students to give examples of a first sentence they could use to begin writing about preparing dinner for their families. Continue asking students for first sentence ideas for the other prompts on the overhead.

Writing Prompts

One way to really understand prompts is to have students write their own. Ask students to write two examples of prompts, one for expository and one for narrative writing, then trade papers with a classmate.

Students should check each others' prompts to be certain all three sections have been included. Have them circle the clue words and determine which prompt is for expository and which one is for narrative writing. Students working together can help each other understand prompts better.

More Prompt Practice

Give students a copy of the prompts activity on page 28 to practice identifying the three parts of a prompt, recognizing and circling clue words, and writing topic sentences.

How to Read and Write Prompts

Your parents have to work late tomorrow evening. They have asked you to prepare dinner for the family.

Before you write, think about how you are going to prepare dinner for the family.

Explain how you are going to prepare dinner for the family.

Eating snacks is fun. Everyone has favorite snacks they like to eat.

Before you begin to write, think of your favorite snack.

Explain why it is your favorite snack.

When you came to school, there was a note on your desk from your teacher telling you that she wasn't going to be at school today. She told you to be in charge for the day.

Before you begin to write, think about what it would be like if you were in charge of your class for a day.

Tell a story about the day you were in charge of your class.

Your family plans to go on vacation in June. They have not decided where to go yet. They have asked for your suggestions about where to go on vacation.

Before you begin writing, think about where you would like to go on a family vacation.

Explain where you think your family should go on vacation.

Most people have a favorite piece of clothing, like a comfortable old shirt, a pair of pants, or a jacket.

Before you begin to write, think about your favorite piece of clothing.

Tell why this piece of clothing is your favorite one.

Everyone talks about the weather, but no one does anything to change the weather.

Before you begin to write, think about what you would change about the weather if you could.

Write a story about how you would change the weather.

Activity: How to Read and Write Prompts

Name: _____

Label each section of the prompts (1, 2, 3). Circle the clue words in each prompt.

> **When you arrive home from school, you find the house is empty.**
> **No one left you a note.**

💡 Before you begin to write, think about why the house is empty.

✏️ Write a story about why the house is empty.

Would you write an expository or narrative essay for this prompt?

_____

Use the clue words to write one sentence for this prompt:

_____

_____

> **You and three friends are in the mood for pizza. Your parents said you**
> **can order one, but everyone wants different toppings on the pizza. It's up**
> **to you to order the pizza.**

💡 Before you begin to write, think about how to order a pizza when everyone wants different toppings on the pizza.

✏️ Explain how you will please everyone who wants different toppings and order the pizza.

Would you write an expository or narrative essay for this prompt?

_____

Use the clue words to write one sentence for this prompt:

_____

_____

 © Good Apple GA1681

Last night you had an unusual dream about being on another planet.

 Before you begin to write, think about what it would be like to be on another planet.

 Write a story about your dream of being on another planet.

Would you write an expository or narrative essay for this prompt?

_____

Use the clue words to write one sentence for this prompt:

_____

_____

EXPOSITORY PROMPT CLUE WORDS

Look for these words in the prompts:

Explain

Tell why

Tell how

© Good Apple GA1681

NARRATIVE
PROMPT CLUE WORDS

 **Look for these words in the prompts:**

Tell a story

Write a story

Tell about

Reproducible

Other Essential Basic Writing Skills

Purpose: To introduce and/or reinforce other essential basic writing skills.

This page can be used in advance of the Student Writing Workshop or as part of the Workshop itself.

Attention Grabbers (visual aid on page 34)

An attention grabber is a sentence before the topic sentence. It should be related to the topic and designed to get the reader interested. By using attention grabbers, students can make their expository writing more interesting. Ask students to give suggestions for opening sentences that would grab the readers' attention.

Transitional Words (visual aid on page 35)

Transitional words help the flow of writing from one paragraph to the next. Students can use words like *first, second,* and *third,* to state reasons or examples. Transitional words are very helpful in the concluding paragraph or sentence of an essay. Ask students for examples of other transitional words.

Instead of Writing Said... (visual aid on page 36)

He said...she said...they said.... After a while, that becomes boring. The visual aid, "Instead of Writing Said..." on page 36 provides students with many alternatives to the word *said.*

The End (visual aid on page 37)

Remind students that when they finish writing, the closing sentence is the end. Writing "The End" is unnecessary.

No Erase (visual aid on page 38)

Rather than erasing when they make a mistake, encourage students to cross out and write the correct word. This makes their writing easier to read.

Proofreading is Essential

Always allow students time to proofread their work before turning it in. Be consistent and insistent on proofreading. Even rough drafts should be proofread and corrected.

Students need to check their spelling, grammar, punctuation, and capitalization. Keep several dictionaries in the classroom for student use.

Students should be encouraged to exchange papers with a classmate and proofread each others' writing after they have done it once themselves. An extra set of eyes never hurts.

Even students using a spelling checker on a computer need to be reminded that not all errors will be found. They must proofread.

Reproducible

ATTENTION GRABBERS

Use funny words!

Write exciting sentences!

Surprise your reader
with your creativity!

Capture you reader's attention
by asking a question!

TRANSITIONAL WORDS

however	although
furthermore	most important
finally	on the other hand
second	therefore
third	meanwhile
last	in summary
next	for instance
in conclusion	in addition
in the meantime	for example
as a result	afterward
above all	briefly
in fact	
on the contrary	
in any event	
certainly	

Instead of Writing Said...

agreed	argued
replied	asked
complained	begged
exclaimed	yelled
added	responded
babbled	ordered
announced	cried
answered	remarked
shouted	reported
whispered	hollered
joked	shrieked

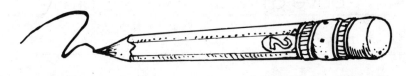

Reproducible

Instead, use a closing or ending sentence

No Erase

Instead, cross out or line out

Reproducible

Focus Scope

Purpose: To help students focus on a topic and write supporting sentences.

This activity can be used during the Student Writer's Workshop or as a follow-up activity after the workshop.

Tell students that the most important step in writing is to stay focused. Encourage students to brainstorm ideas to these questions:

 Why it is important to stay focused when writing?

 What happens when a writer doesn't stay focused?

Introduce this activity by telling them: Today we are going to make and use something that will help us remember how important it is to stay focused.

Have students roll up a piece of paper into the shape of a tube, tape the edges, and decorate it with writing terms. This will be their "Focus Scope."

Tell students to look around the room with their Focus Scopes. Have them focus on objects in the room and look at their peers.

After several minutes, ask students to focus on one object in the room. Write the name of the object on a piece of paper. This will be a topic. Do this five times.

When they have written five topics, have students go back to the first topic and look at it again with their Focus Scopes. This time, ask them to write three details about this topic.

Do this for each of the five topics they focused on. When they are done, ask students:

 How does this activity reinforce previous writing skills you have learned?

 How does focusing on and writing about details help you with writing?

Give students additional practice by writing the word *ROBIN* on the board. Read the sentences on page 40. Ask students whether each sentence focuses on the topic. If it does not, ask why not?

ROBIN

Robins are a sign of spring.
Birds fly south for the winter.
Robins eat worms.
My friend's name is Robin.
Robin Hood was a famous character in many stories.
Robin eggs are blue.
Robins build nests in trees.
Some birds build nests on the ground.
Ducks can swim, but robins can't.

I Spy Riddle Game

Purpose: To reinforce writing concepts learned.

This activity can be used during the Student Writer's Workshop and/or at other times during the year.

At the end of the Student Writer's Workshop, students can play the "I Spy" riddle game to reinforce the concepts and skills they learned. This game requires students to pay close attention to the text of the visuals displayed. As they analyze the visuals looking for riddle ideas, poster information is reinforced.

Tell students that they will be asked to make up an "I Spy" riddle for the class. They need to find a word or phrase on one of the writing-related posters and offer a clue to the word's identity.

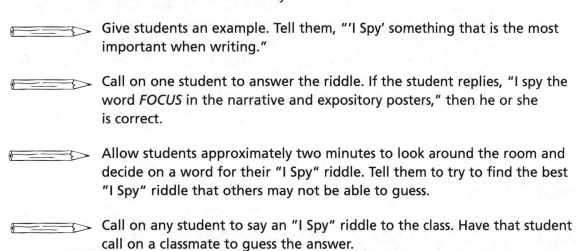

Give students an example. Tell them, "'I Spy' something that is the most important when writing."

Call on one student to answer the riddle. If the student replies, "I spy the word *FOCUS* in the narrative and expository posters," then he or she is correct.

Allow students approximately two minutes to look around the room and decide on a word for their "I Spy" riddle. Tell them to try to find the best "I Spy" riddle that others may not be able to guess.

Call on any student to say an "I Spy" riddle to the class. Have that student call on a classmate to guess the answer.

As students play "I Spy" throughout the year, they review and reinforce the writing concepts they learned.

A variation of this game would be to give students a few minutes to look around the room for a topic for expository or narrative writing. This could be an item on a poster, an object in the room, or something they see out the window. They can use their focus scopes to select a topic.

An appropriate clue would be for a student to say, "'I Spy' something that would make a good topic for a narrative about a trip to the zoo."

Other students could try to focus on the item mentioned to answer the "I Spy" riddle. This can generate ideas for writing topics as well as sharpen students' observational skills. Playing "I Spy" increases students' awareness that they are surrounded by ideas for writing topics.

Paper Bag Topic Game

Purpose: To give students opportunities for spontaneous writing.

This activity can be used during the Student Writer's Workshop and/or at other times during the year.

Materials

You will need one paper lunch bag for each group of four or five students. Write topics on small pieces of paper and put five to ten topics in each bag.

Divide the class into groups of four or five. Give each group a paper bag with the small pieces of paper inside. Tell students that on the count of three they should reach into the bag and take out one piece of paper. Ask them to read the topic and write the first three ideas about that topic that come to mind.

When they finish writing, ask them to return the paper to the bag. On the count of three, they can reach into the bag and select a different topic. Again, ask them to write the first three ideas that come to mind about that topic. After doing this several times, call on students to share what they wrote.

You can photocopy the ideas on page 43 for topics and cut them out or make up your own.

Paper Bag Topics

A day at the beach	What's for dinner?
A starry night	Getting lost
Hiking in the woods	Preparing a pizza
The smell of flowers	An unusual breakfast
A thunderstorm	A blustery day
Flowers in the desert	A pair of scuffed shoes
A snow-covered mountain	Mowing the lawn
At the bottom of the ocean	Autumn
A family trip	Spring fever
Birds	A blizzard
A baseball game	Building a fort
Shopping at a mall	A trip to another city
Your community	Summertime
A trip to the dentist	An arcade or video game
My favorite book	My favorite movie
My family	The best pet

Exciting and Fun Ways to Practice Formal Writing

Purpose: The writing activities on the following pages are designed to provide students with an opportunity to apply the writing skills they learned.

The following activities offer students opportunities to self-evaluate and for you to assess and make observations about their writing. They can be used as part of the Student Writer's Workshop or as follow-up activities. Students need feedback to improve. Be sure to offer praise for what they are doing right as well as suggestions on how to improve.

By providing two prompts for each assignment, students have an opportunity to choose which style, expository or narrative, they feel most comfortable writing. If a student consistently chooses the same style of writing, and some will, you will know that particular student needs more help with the other type of writing. This gives you another opportunity to assist students in the areas where they need the most guidance.

Students will practice both types of writing on a variety of topics by participating in the group writing experience described below.

Rotating Group Paragraphs

1. Divide students into cooperative groups of five.

2. Ask each student to write a topic sentence of his or her choice on a piece of paper.

3. At your signal, have students pass their papers to the right. After they read the topic sentence, ask them to write one supporting sentence.

4. Again, have students pass their papers to the right. Have them read the topic sentence and supporting sentence, then add one more supporting sentence.

5. Repeat Step 4 twice more.

6. On the final rotation, students will have their original topic sentences back with four supporting sentences written by other members of the class. Students should then write a concluding sentence.

7. Ask groups to share their writing by reading some of their paragraphs to the class. Students could illustrate their group paragraphs and display them in the classroom.

8. Combine group paragraphs into a class book and make a copy for each student.

Other practice ideas include "The Great Pet Escape" on page 46, "What's Inside the Hat?" on page 48, "A Toy Character Story" on page 49. You'll find "Story Starters" on page 56 and more Sample Prompts on page 54.

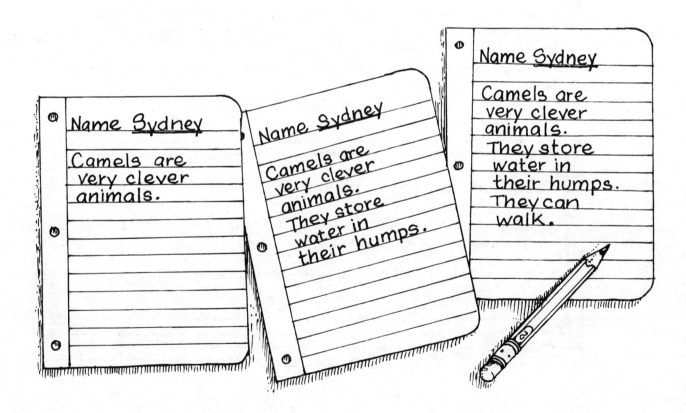

The Great Pet Escape

If you have a classroom pet, then this activity is for you! Kids are motivated to write as they imagine where their class pet may have gone and what adventures it is experiencing.

While students are out of the room, hide the classroom pet in your room or take it to another classroom.

Write on the carpet with sidewalk chalk that the class pet is missing. It could be something like, "Oh no! _____ is missing. Where could he be?" Have large X marks leading from the cage to other areas of the room where the class pet could have disappeared.

When students return to the room, act surprised about the pet's disappearance.

Tell students they have to find their class pet. In order to find it, they must come up with an organized plan. This is when you introduce the prompts. (Students will probably catch on that this was preplanned! This is where your acting skills are most important!)

Provide two prompts for students to use to write about where the class pet might be or how to find it.

Read the prompts out loud or write them on the board.

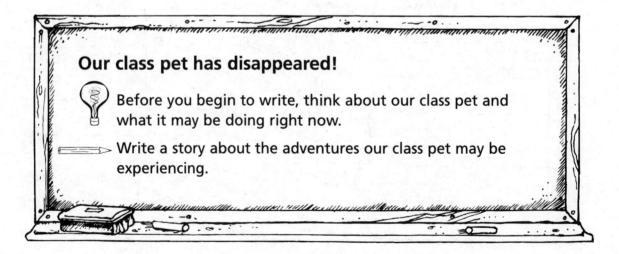

Our class pet has disappeared!

Before you begin to write, think about our class pet and what it may be doing right now.

Write a story about the adventures our class pet may be experiencing.

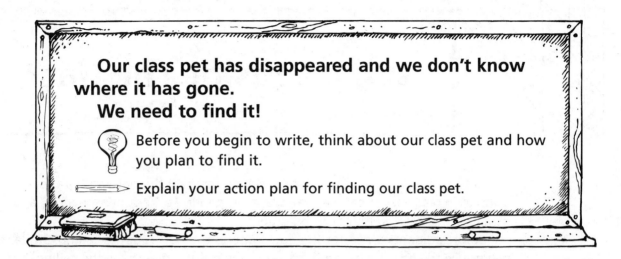

Our class pet has disappeared and we don't know where it has gone.
We need to find it!

Before you begin to write, think about our class pet and how you plan to find it.

Explain your action plan for finding our class pet.

Tell students that they can use either prompt. Review expository and narrative writing skills if necessary.

When they complete their rough drafts, ask for volunteers to read their plans or stories about the class pet out loud.

To relieve any anxiety, retrieve the class pet after the activity is completed and return it to its home.

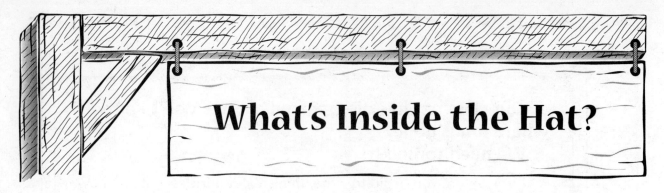

What's Inside the Hat?

Bring or make a large hat. You could use a cowboy hat, a sombrero, a Santa hat, a top hat, a football helmet, or a silly bonnet. Fill the hat with wrapped goodies in plain paper or seasonal wrapping paper. Stickers, pens, pencils, and other writing related items can be used.

Before students arrive for the day, suspend the hat from the ceiling. Students will notice the hat and be curious about why it is hanging from the ceiling. They will wonder what is inside it. Let their curiosity grow by not explaining the activity right away. Instead, go ahead with your lessons as scheduled. That will build excitement about the writing assignment later.

When you are ready to begin the writing lesson, provide two prompts for students to use. Read them out loud or write them on the board.

Review narrative and expository writing skills before students begin to write.

When you walked into the classroom this morning, there was a hat hanging from the ceiling. It looks like something is in the hat.

Before you begin to write, imagine what could be inside the hat.

Write a story about what you think is inside the hat.

When you walked into the classroom this morning, there was a hat hanging from the ceiling. It looks like something is in the hat.

Before you begin to write, think about what is in the hat.

Explain what you think is in the hat.

Tell students they can use either prompt for the writing activity.

When they have completed the rough draft, have students share their writing. See if anyone guessed what was in the hat. When they finish, reveal what the hat contains and share the goodies with the class.

A Toy Character Story

Make copies of the parent letter on page 50 and send it home with students the day before you plan to use this writing activity.

When students arrive for the day, let them put their stuffed animal or toy figurine in view until it's time to write. Allow students to ask each other questions about that toy and why it is special. This will start them thinking about the topic.

When you are ready to begin the writing lesson, provide two prompts for students to use. Read them out loud or write them on the board.

When you came home from school you found your favorite toy had come to life.

 Before you begin to write, think about the fun day you and your toy will have together.

Write a story about your toy coming to life and what you did.

When you were playing with your toy, all of a sudden it came to life!

 Before you begin writing, think about how your toy came to life.

Explain how you think your toy came to life.

Tell students they can use either prompt for the writing activity. When they have finished the rough draft, ask volunteers to share their writing and their toy with the class.

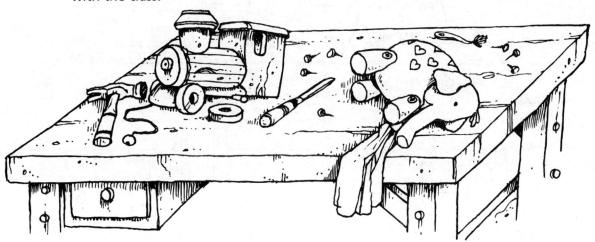

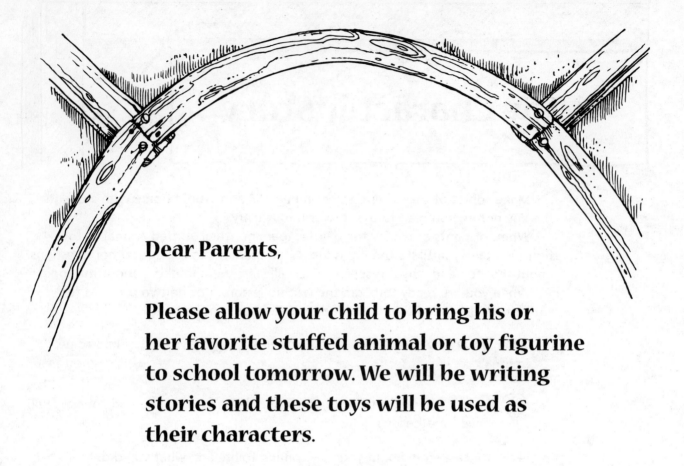

Dear Parents,

Please allow your child to bring his or her favorite stuffed animal or toy figurine to school tomorrow. We will be writing stories and these toys will be used as their characters.

Thank you,

_____

My Favorite Toys

Reproducible

Students as Teachers

Purpose: To allow students an opportunity to present a summary of what they learned about writing and to review and reinforce what was taught during the Student Writer's Workshop.

This can be used as a follow-up after a Student Writer's Workshop.

After spending all the time and energy preparing and presenting the Student Writer's Workshop, you deserve a break. You're probably ready to step back and let someone else take over for a while. This activity allows you to do exactly that.

Tell students you are too "worn out" from all the talking about writing at the Student Writer's Workshop. You are ready for a break. Ask the class for volunteers to take your place as teacher. Most students are eager for a chance to be the teacher. Inform them that it's their lucky day. Everyone will have a chance to be the teacher for a short time during the next week.

Tell students that for a teacher to teach, he or she must prepare first. Teachers must know what they are going to teach, have a plan for teaching it, and prepare the materials they will need for presenting the lesson.

Divide students into cooperative groups of three or four to prepare and create a presentation. Supply paper, crayons, overhead transparencies, markers, staplers, glue, scissors, etc., for students to use in preparing their presentations.

Tell students that they will need to make a booklet of what they learned about writing at the Student Writer's Workshop for their teaching presentation. Their booklets need to be organized, neat, colorful, and accurate. Their booklets are the main requirement and will be used as their main teaching tool.

Once the booklet is complete, the group can add other materials to use in their presentation, like posters, overheads, and writing activities for the class.

Give students a definite time frame for their presentations. Allow plus or minus two minutes, but try to have them keep within the allotted time. Planning their time for the presentation is important. Ask each group to sign up for a day to give their presentation.

On each assigned day, a different group will be the teacher for the day during writing time. Students will present their booklets and any other materials they have.

Participate in the activities presented by the group. Students will enjoy seeing their teacher in the role of student. As groups present their material, the class has an opportunity to review what they learned. Allow a five minute question-and-answer period after each presentation. Use the opportunity to ask higher level questions of the student teachers.

52

Night Writes!

Night Writes! is a take-home writing assignment. After you have taught all the skills and concepts necessary to write fluent and accurate text, provide students with independent practice at home. While they are writing at home without any help from the teacher, they will realize where they really need assistance. Often students depend on the help they receive from the teacher and they don't rely on themselves. Each day after the take-home assignment, the teacher needs to provide time to assist students who had difficulty the night before. Sharing time also needs to be provided.

Have students staple five pieces of writing paper to the back of a blank sheet of paper. Have them title their cover page, "Night Writes," and write their name on the cover.

As a group, select what topics to write about for the next week's homework. After the topics are selected, have the students write the topics in their booklets, one topic per page.

Model with the students how you expect them to write the assignments.

Remind them to read the prompt correctly, making sure to look for clue words. Suggest they brainstorm with classmates or family members for ideas.

Remind students to use the correct graphic organizer and to apply all skills and concepts learned in class.

The Sample Prompts on pages 54 and 55 and Story Starters on page 56 can provide many topic ideas.

Remember to provide time the next school day to conference with any students that need assistance.

Sample Prompts

Everyone loves to have a great day.

Before you begin to write, think about a day you had that was great.

Tell about that day and explain what made it such a great day.

Everyone has something or someone special in his or her life.

Before you begin to write, think about that special something or someone in your life.

Tell about and explain why that something or someone is special to you.

Summer is here and school is out!

Before you begin to write, think about what your parents would say if your report card did not have good grades.

Explain what you think your parents would say to you.

All students have their own thoughts on how they feel about school.

Before you begin to write, think about how you feel about school.

Explain how you feel about school.

Narrative Prompts

There are many times when something funny happens.

Before you begin to write, think about a time when something funny happened to you.

Tell a story about something you thought was very funny.

Lots of people like to shop for new things.

Before you begin to write, imagine winning a shopping spree and being able to shop at any store and buy anything you want.

Tell about the store where you would shop and what you would buy.

Surprises sure are fun!

Before you begin writing, imagine finding a large brown bag sitting in the middle of the floor when you got home from school.

Tell a story about what you think is in the bag.

Stormy weather sometimes happens during a school day.

Before you begin to write, think about what would happen if a storm caused the electricity to go out while you were at school.

Tell a story about what you think the day at school would be like without electricity.

It's Friday night and the weekend is here. You don't have any homework. Your parents said you could do anything you want to this weekend.

Before you begin to write, think about what you would like to do.

Tell a story about your fun weekend.

Story Starters

Sometimes students run into a temporary writing block. Then the most difficult part of writing becomes choosing the topic. These suggestions can be used to generate ideas for class activities or take-home assignments.

 Have students bring in a favorite picture and use that as a writing topic.

 Let students look through magazines and cut out pictures that they think would be interesting writing topics.

 To make pictures more interesting, let students cut out parts of several pictures and combine them to create a completely new scene.

Remind students that they will be writing narrative text if they write a story about the pictures. They will be writing expository text if they explain or describe the pictures.

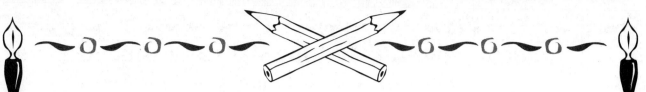

More Story Starter Topics to Generate Ideas

If I wrote the Constitution

What the American flag means to me

Traveling west in the 1800's

Living in colonial times

Being the U.S. President for a day

Exploring unknown land

Being patriotic means...

Someday, I would like...

A family holiday memory

Walking on the moon

Life on another planet

A journey through the solar system

The universe

But really, I didn't...

What I found under the stairs

I am a good pet owner because...

Why you should spay or neuter your pet

Adopting a shelter pet

Animals in circuses are sad because...

How I take care of my pet

Wild animals aren't good pets

My favorite amusement park ride

Earth day is...

I recycle because...

What I can do to take care of the Earth

My best friend

I admire...

My favorite holiday memory

I am special because...

I am best at...

A hot air balloon ride

My favorite subject in school

Student Expository Writing Skills Assessment

Student Name: _____

Date(s) of Assessment: _____

Use the following key to assess samples of student writing. Write the date and circle the appropriate number in a different color each time you assess student work.

1 Student has not mastered this skill at all yet.

2 Student demonstrates a slight understanding of this skill.

3 Student demonstrates a basic understanding of this skill, but needs additional practice.

4 Student displays understanding and some mastery of this skill.

5 Student has mastered this skill.

1 2 3 4 5   Restates the prompt.

1 2 3 4 5   Writes text that is focused on the prompt.

1 2 3 4 5   Realizes that expository writing is a five-paragraph essay:
• introduction
• 3 supporting paragraphs
• conclusion

1 2 3 4 5   Writes a five-paragraph essay with an introductory paragraph that includes:
• a restatement of the prompt.
• an attention-grabber written before the topic sentence.
• a statement of what the supporting paragraphs are about.

1 2 3 4 5   Writes a good topic sentence.

1 2 3 4 5   Writes a five-paragraph essay with at least three detailed supporting paragraphs.

1 2 3 4 5   Writes at least three supporting paragraphs about the topic.

1 2 3 4 5   Writes a five-paragraph essay that includes a concluding paragraph summarizing the topic.

1 2 3 4 5   Writes a concluding sentence.

1 2 3 4 5   Uses correct grammar, capitalization, and punctuation.

1 2 3 4 5   Uses vivid verbs and strong adjectives properly.

1 2 3 4 5   Uses transitional words properly.

1 2 3 4 5   Recognizes and identifies the differences between expository and narrative writing.

Items to praise:

_____

_____

_____

_____

_____

_____

Items to work on with the student:

_____

_____

_____

_____

_____

_____

Student Narrative Writing Skills Assessment

Student Name: _____

Date(s) of Assessment: _____

Use the following key to assess samples of student writing. Write the date and circle the appropriate number in a different color each time you assess student work.

1 Student has not mastered this skill at all yet.

2 Student demonstrates a slight understanding of this skill.

3 Student demonstrates a basic understanding of this skill, but needs additional practice.

4 Student displays understanding and some mastery of this skill.

5 Student has mastered this skill.

---

1 2 3 4 5   Restates the prompt.

1 2 3 4 5   Writes text that is focused on the prompt.

1 2 3 4 5   Realizes that narrative writing should follow the same components that "real books" have, i.e., a beginning, middle, end, setting, and characters.

1 2 3 4 5   Writes a beginning paragraph that introduces and describes the characters and setting and includes characters' motives and feelings.

1 2 3 4 5   Writes a clear beginning sentence that introduces characters and setting.

1 2 3 4 5   Writes middle paragraphs that introduce the problem or action and use descriptive writing.

1 2 3 4 5   Writes three or more middle sentences that define the problem or show action.

1 2 3 4 5   Writes an ending that has a conclusion and provides a solution to the problem.

1 2 3 4 5   Writes a clear ending sentence that includes a conclusion or solution.

1 2 3 4 5   Uses proper grammar, capitalization, and punctuation.

1 2 3 4 5   Uses vivid verbs and strong adjectives properly.

1 2 3 4 5   Uses transitional words properly.

1 2 3 4 5   Recognizes and identifies the differences between expository and narrative text writing.

Reproducible

Items to praise:

_____

_____

_____

_____

_____

_____

Items to work on with the student:

_____

_____

_____

_____

_____

_____

End-of-the-Year Writing Expectations:

General Writing Skills

Grade level 1	2	3	4	5	At the end of the year, students should be able to do the following, based on grade level:
X	X	X	X	X	Respond to a prompt with a topic picture.
X	X	X	X	X	Write words to describe pictures, using sound spellings.
X	X	X	X	X	Recognize familiar writing terms: topic, sentence, narrative, paragraph, text, main idea, and prompt.
	X	X	X	X	Recognize and identify the differences between expository and narrative text writing.
	X	X	X		Understand that creative writing and formal writing are different.
		X	X		Identify the three sections of a prompt.
	X	X	X		Use grammar, capitalization and punctuation correctly.
X	X	X	X	X	Use exciting vocabulary words properly.
X	X	X	X	X	Include many accurate details.
	X	X	X	X	Use vivid verbs and strong adjectives properly.
	X	X	X		Proper use of transition words.
X	X	X	X	X	Listen to a prompt and write at least three sentences about the prompt.
X	X	X	X	X	Write in a sequential and organized manner.
		X	X		Successfully read a prompt and write text that is focused on the prompt.

Reproducible

End-of-the-Year Writing Expectations:

Expository Writing Skills

Grade level 1 2 3 4 5	At the end of the year, students should be able to do the following, based on grade level:
X X X X	Write a good topic sentence.
X X X X	Write at least three supporting sentences about a topic.
X X X X X	Write a paragraph that includes: • a good topic sentence • three supporting sentences • at least one sentence describing each of the supporting sentences • a concluding sentence
X X	Write a five-paragraph essay which includes: • an introduction • three supporting paragraphs • a conclusion
X X	Write an introductory paragraph which includes: • a restatement of the prompt • an attention-grabber written before the topic sentence • a statement of what the three supporting paragraphs are about
X X	Write at least three detailed paragraphs.
X X	Write a concluding paragraph.
X X	Use transitional words properly.

End-of-the-Year Writing Expectations:

Narrative Writing Skills

Grade level 1 2 3 4 5	At the end of the year, students should be able to do the following, based on grade level:
X X X X X	Realize that writing should follow guidelines, i.e., have a beginning, middle, ending, characters and setting.
X X X	Write a clear beginning, middle, and ending which include the following: • beginning: introduce characters and setting • middle: create the problem or action • ending: include a conclusion or solution
X X	Properly develop a beginning, middle and ending. (Guidelines for each are listed below.)
X X	Develop a beginning that • introduces and describes the characters and setting • includes characters' motives and feelings
X X	Write middle paragraphs that introduce the problem or action and use descriptive writing.
X X	Write an ending that • has a conclusion • provides a solution to the problem
X X	Use transitional words properly.

Reproducible